LORD
AND HIS

ROSIE   HAIRPIN HUGGINS   SKINNY LIZZIE

MARMADUKE, the young Lord of Bunkerton, known to his friends and to generations of comic readers as Lord Snooty, made his debut appearance in the first issue of a new comic paper, "The Beano", on July 30th, 1938, many years before current superstar Dennis the Menace. That first edition, sixty years ago, would be barely recognisable alongside today's Beano. Mainly black and white throughout, it was a mixture of illustrated text stories, full page comic stories and shorter comic strips. Funny business with Big Eggo, the cover star in those early days, was mixed with action and adventure from the likes of Morgyn the Mighty.

Issue 1 of The Beano, featuring Big Eggo on the cover, is a lot different to today's issues.

SNOOTY PALS

SCRAPPER SMITH   "HAPPY" HUTTON   GERTIE THE GOAT

Artist Dudley D. Watkins drew himself into one episode of Lord Snooty.

"The Beano" was launched to follow in the successful wake of "The Dandy", which had first appeared on December 4th the previous year. It was no surprise that it made use of its sister comic's talented artists, including Dudley Dexter Watkins, who not only drew the weekly adventures of Desperate Dan in "The Dandy", but also provided illustrations for adventure papers like "The Rover". Watkins' task in the new comic was to create the visuals for the newest member of the House of Lords, Lord Snooty himself.

In the early strips, the responsibilities of being a peer of the realm weighed heavily on Snooty's young shoulders and he would slip into disguise to mix with his pals from Ash Can Alley. It wasn't long before the Ash Can Alley kids came up against their most bitter rivals, the Gasworks Gang. Other adventures involved the eccentric Professor Screwtop and his even more eccentric inventions. Snooty and pals could usually be relied upon to test these new inventions.

Although everything in Bunkerton Castle was fun and games, world events were to provide the scriptwriters with a new theme, as Snooty and pals entered the propaganda battle in the early stages of the Second World War. Over the following years, the pals would repel many a Nazi assault on Bunkerton Castle and Lord Snooty often ended up personally taking on the Fuhrer and his High Command.

THE GASWORKS GANG

With the war over, Snooty and his pals returned to their more usual business of having fun, punctuated with the odd pitched battle with the Gasworks Gang. Dudley D. Watkins continued to draw the strip until April 1968, although, during the 1950's and 1960's he had also been joined on art chores by other illustrators.

This then, is —

THE LEGEND OF LORD SNOOTY AND HIS PALS...

LORD SNOOTY AND HIS PALS

The Beano July 30th, 1938.

Lord Snooty's plan is just the ticket—
for a game which certainly isn't cricket!

The Beano August 6th, 1938.

At Snooty's ball, the swells and swanks— cheer the Alley Gang for their alley pranks.

The Beano August 13th, 1938.

The Castle Cook's pie was a real beauty—
before being filled by the gang and Snooty!

The Beano August 27th, 1938.

His Lordship appears to be on a winner
when the gang are invited round for dinner!

To animals, teacher couldn't be sweeter—
till Snooty brought the zoo to meet her.

His worship faces a terrible blow–
when he decrees the removal of Bunkerton's snow.

The Beano December 17th, 1938.

The solution calls for something drastic–
to solve a problem most gymnastic.

The Beano January 21st, 1939.

Lord Marmaduke's men of entertainment—
keep the task within containment.

The Beano March 25th, 1939.

The men of ice have dreams of booty,
but they're no match for bold Lord Snooty.

The Beano September 16th, 1939.

To his Lordship, one must hand it, he makes a splendid Mexican bandit.

The Beano September 23rd, 1939.

16

His Lordship's plans of jig and prance– lead MacDuff a merry dance!

THE WAR YEARS

ON January 6th, 1940 the first Lord Snooty mentioning the war was printed. Over the next few years, Lord Snooty's stories were to feature the war more than any other D. C. Thomson comic strip.

They often covered the topics of rationing, shortages and air-raids. One strip particularly mentioned the wearing of gas masks — a reminder to children of the importance of carrying them.

Shortages and rationing affected everyone. We often see Snooty and his gang collecting their BEANOS from the newsagent and this was another reminder for readers. If you didn't have your comic on order, you couldn't get one! As paper shortages became even worse, many comics began to be printed fortnightly instead of weekly.

Many other Lord Snooty storylines featured the war effort, bombing and Hitler's propaganda campaigns. The gang even helped to catch German spies. One thing was for sure though, no matter how clever Herr Hitler thought he was, he could never get the better of Snooty and co!

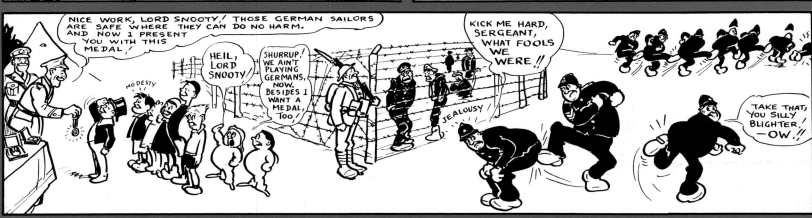

The Beano January 6th, 1940.

His Lordship's plant's in no condition to win the gardening competition.

The Beano February 24th, 1940.

A brand new football and lots of tuck—
but then the gang run out of luck.

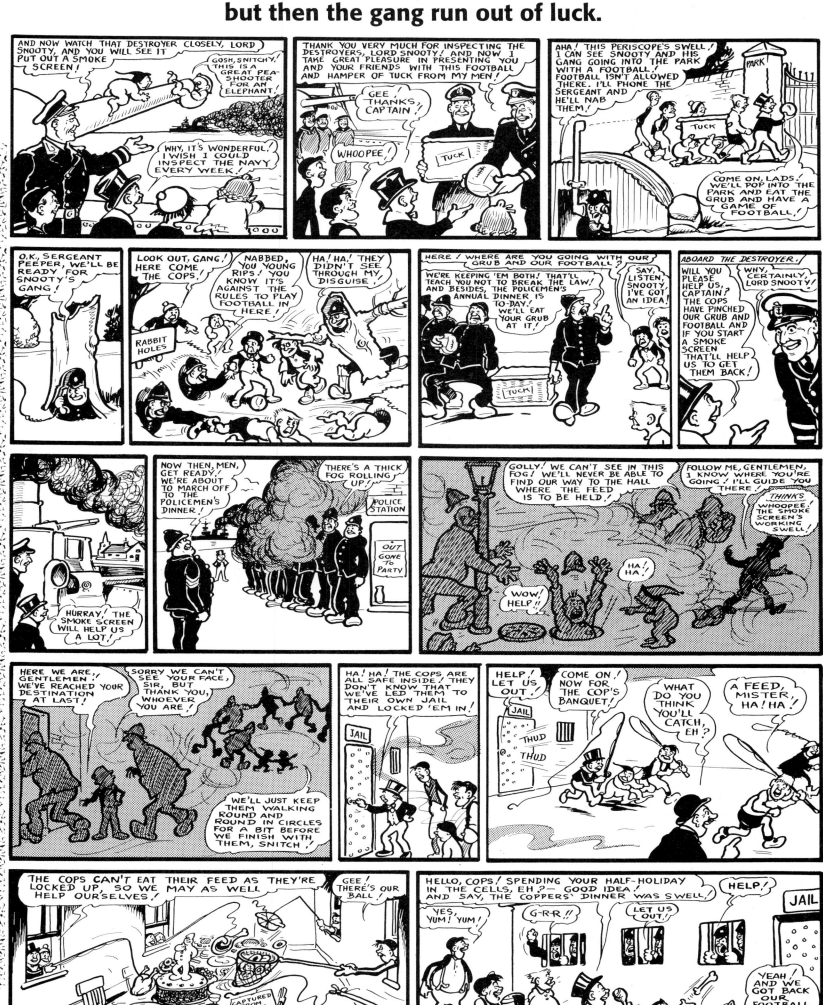

Lord Snooty's on a sure fire winner
when hungry moths go seeking dinner.

A fine idea, Lord Snooty feels— was training these performing seals.

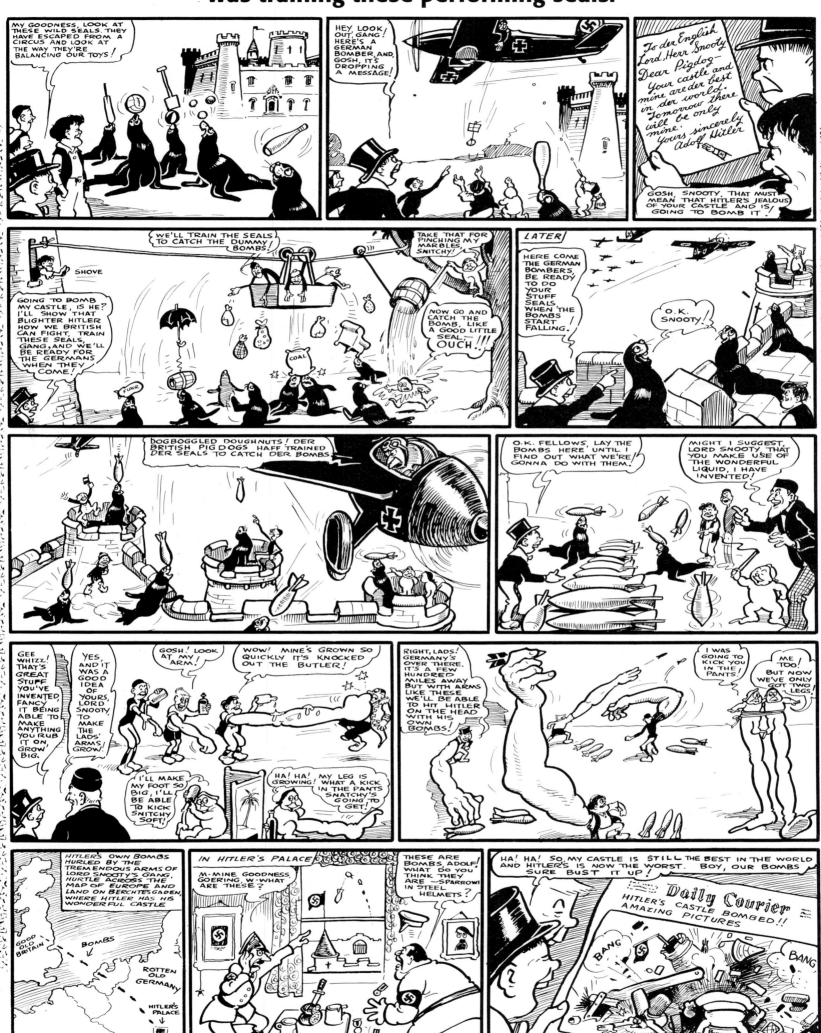

The Beano August 10th, 1940.

The Professor and his picture show—
cause these germs to grow, grow, grow.

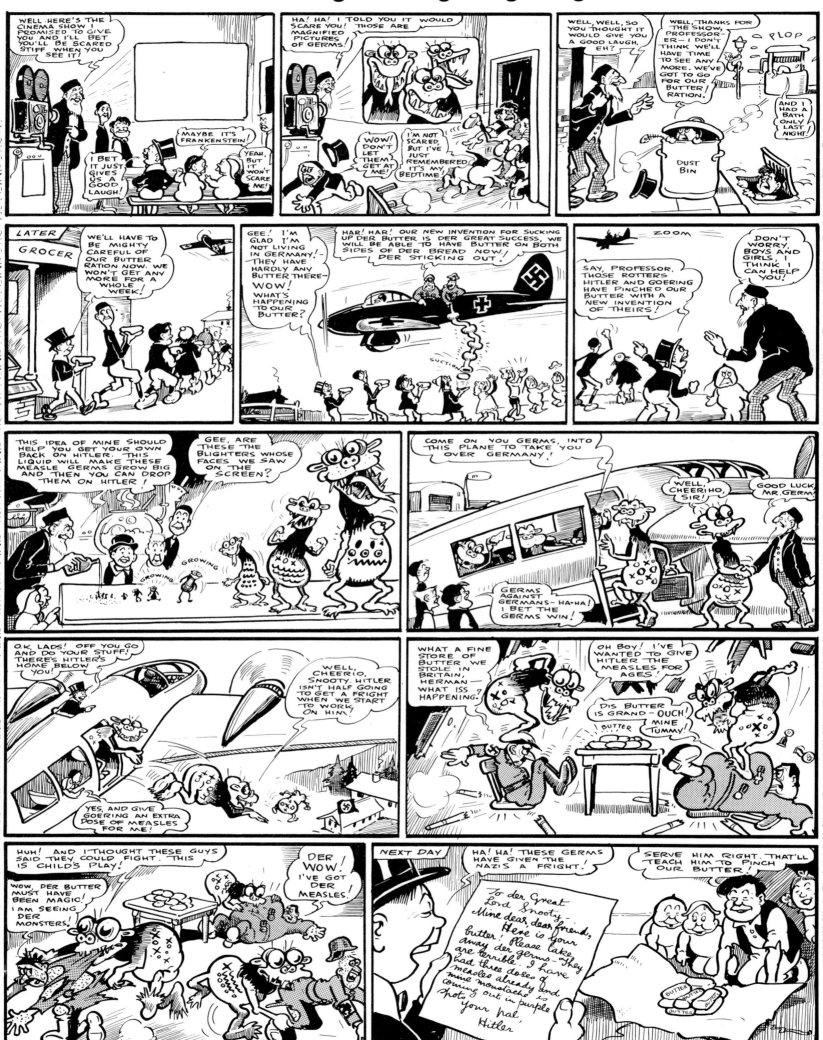

Snooty and his gang all get together with elephants, to provide the weather.

The paper shortage, let us note—
is really getting Snooty's goat.

The Beano October 26th, 1940.

The men of Bunkerton's Home Guard must see Snooty's identity card.

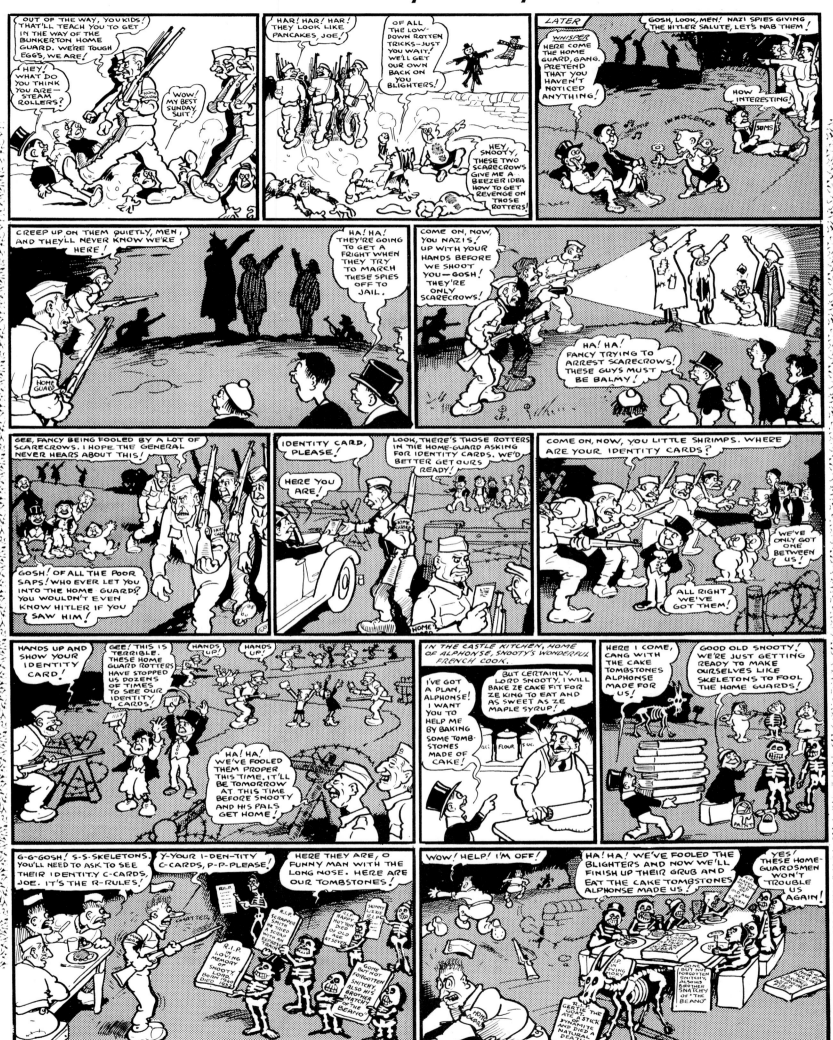

And now the action never pauses—
with a squad of phoney Santa Clauses.

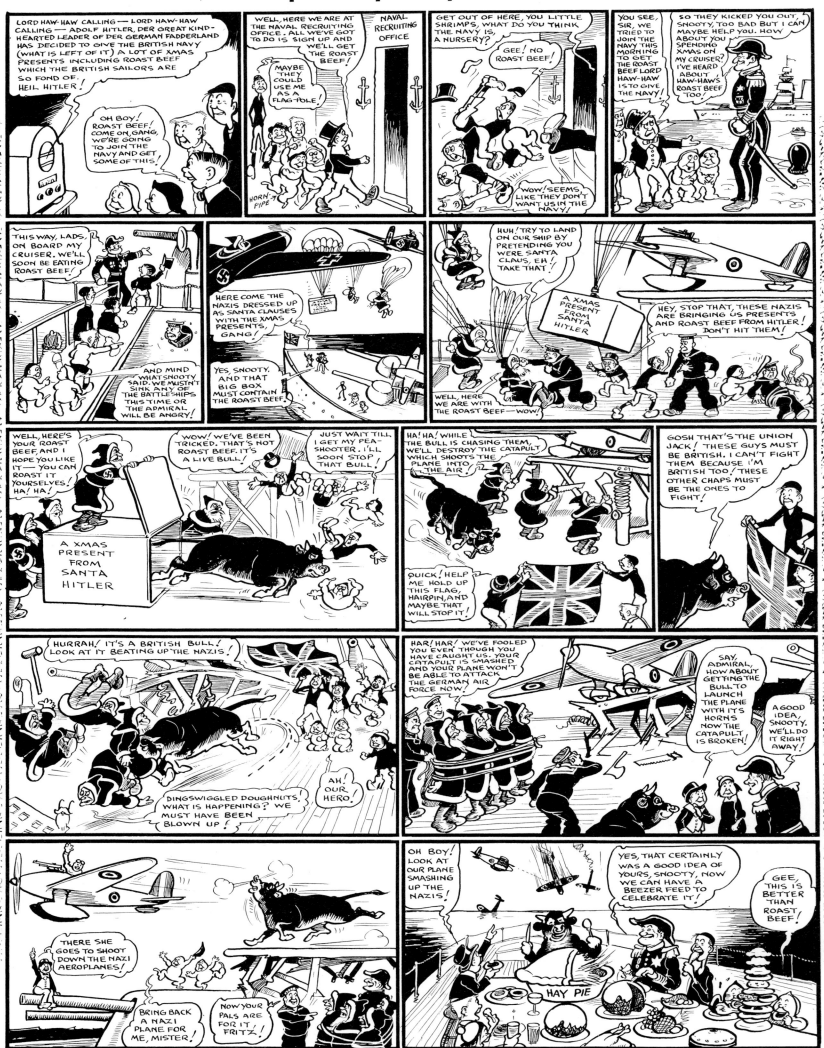

1. LORD SNOOTY and his pals are absolute record-breakers when it comes to spending pocket-money. So they're always on the look-out for a way of earning a copper or three. The other day, outside the Zoo, they saw a notice that pleased them. "Baby-sitters wanted," said the notice. "That's us," said our little lord, thinking the baby-sitters would be wanted for some of the attendants' babies. "We'll take the job!"

2. But when Snooty and his pals applied for the vacant jobs, they soon wished they hadn't been so rash. The baby-sitters were wanted to look after baby hippos! Their Ma was going out to the vet. The keeper led her off, leaving Snooty and company in complete charge of the babies. All the hippos were down in the dumps, too. They wanted to go with their Ma — the big soft babies!

3. The outsize babies were upset. They wept buckets. "If anyone hears them bawling like that we'll be arrested and charged with cruelty to animals," grumbled Snooty. "We'll have to try and stop them. Come on!" The Gang hunted around and found baby bottles, baby clothes and prams big enough to carry baby hippos. Then they started to mother the big kiddies. But it didn't go down well with the hippo kids.

continued on page 39

29

Poor old Bunkerton Castle, alas, suffers from a lack of glass.

Through the skies watch Snooty zoom— on a giant flying broom.

Snooty and the gang, it must be said—
do not approve of rough first aid.

His Lordship helps a kangaroo— recover from a dose of flu.

The Beano March 29th, 1941.

It looks like Snooty has to settle— for Easter eggs of solid metal.

Here's how Lord Snooty's own canteen— became the finest ever seen.

His Lordship is a useful guy— when one wants to find a spy.

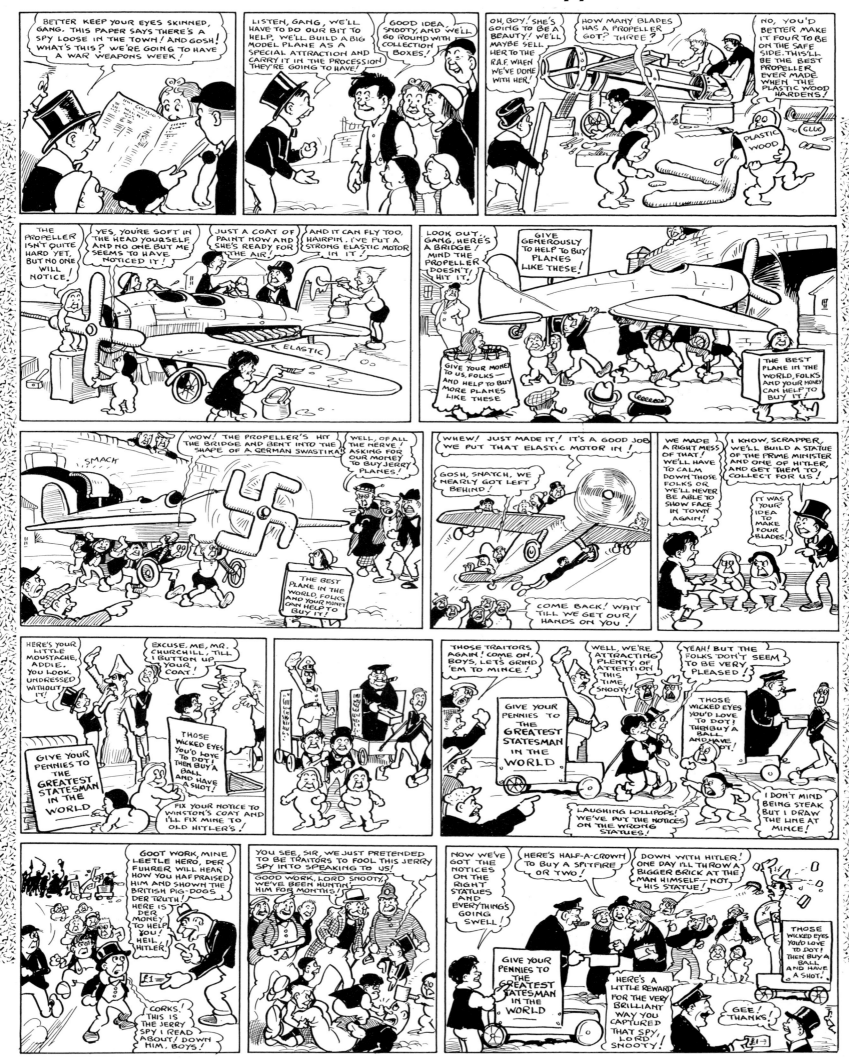

The Beano May 17th, 1941.

Snooty and the gang are doing fine—
down at the bottom of the new coal mine.

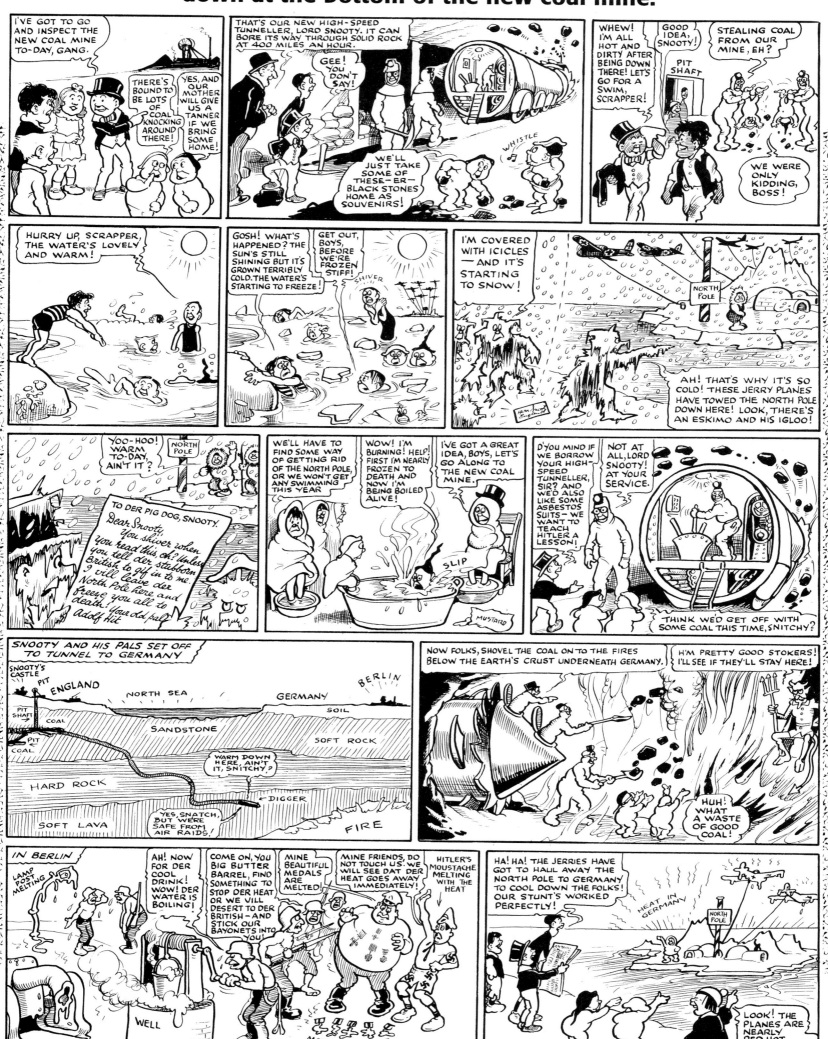

Old Man Winter loses Jack Frost—
but Snooty knows that all's not lost.

The Beano December 20th, 1941.

continued from page 29

continued from page 29

4. "Gosh!" said Snitch. "Me and Snatch have nearly broken our legs trying to bounce a hippo on our knees. It's no good." "We've still got to stop them crying!" declared Snooty. "Remember we'll get no pay if the keeper comes back and finds them unhappy. I know. Let's do tricks." So the Gang started to make faces, tell jokes and do tricks. But, oh dear, the hippos looked glummer still.

5. The hippos did stop crying, however. The Gang's tricks had made them wild instead of glum. They lowered their heads and charged. Bang! Biff! Ouch! "Oh, golly!" groaned Scrapper. "Some people throw tomatoes when they don't like a show. That would be better than this." No wonder Scrapper groused. A baby hippo had his shirt sleeves in its jaws and was shaking him to and fro. Tough luck on Scrapper!

6. At last Snooty thought he had a good plan to help make friends with the young hippos. "Come on, Gang," he said. "We're going somewhere. Not you," he added to Snitch and Snatch, who were still being attacked by the hippos. "You've got to stay here and look after the babies. We don't want to be accused of neglecting them." Poor Snitchy and Snatchy! "Help!" roared Snatch.

continued on page 58

The finer points of art and line—
do suit his Lordship's grand design.

The Beano January 3rd, 1942.

You'll see his Lordship's latest caper— is gathering tons of old waste paper.

The Beano January 17th, 1942.

Lord Snooty and his gallant band— travel to an ancient land.

The Beano January 31st, 1942.

The situation appears alarming—
when Snitch and Snatch become most charming.

The Beano February 14th, 1942.

Who's the girl behind the mask— the Bunkerton gang don't have to ask.

The Beano March 14th, 1942.

When Snooty invents a brand new diet—
his Uncle Alec has to try it.

The Beano October 10th, 1942.

Very soon the light of day— is hidden by a long dark ray.

LORD SNOOTY
AND HIS PALS

When Snooty buys some rubber bricks —

GOSH! Bunkerton Castle, where Lord Snooty and his pals stay, is the place for fun. There's always something happening there. The days nothing happens, Aunt Mat sends for the doctor, thinking the boys and girls must be feeling poorly. Well, only the other day there was something extra funny going on. Snooty had been given a double helping of pocket money for being a good boy two days in succession. And he'd used it all buying a cheap load of rubber bricks. You should have seen these bricks bounce. What's more, being hit with them was like being clubbed by a feather. These rubber bricks certainly were full of tricks and no mistake!

"Come on!" said Snooty, after he'd played about with the bricks for a while. "Let's show these to our pals in town!"

So off they all went with an armful of bouncy bricks. Their luck was out! The first boys they met weren't chums of theirs. They were the Gasworks Gang!

But as the Gasworkers dashed forward to have a fight, Big Fat Joe had a super idea. "Start hitting each other with rubber bricks, Gang!" he hissed.

The Gang caught on and began heaving the bricks about! The Gaswork bullies thought the bricks were real — just as Big Fat Joe had planned!

Off went the Gasworkers! They weren't going to stand up to tough boys and girls who didn't even blink when they were hit by bricks. Not likely! "Ho, ho!" laughed Snooty. "Three cheers for us!"

But Scrapper had a feeling the Gasworks boys would discover they'd been properly diddled.

Snooty had the answer to that. "Build a wall with the rubber bricks, chums!" he said. "Then we'll be ready to repel the invaders if they come back!"

So the gang built a rubber wall — and just in time, too. The Gasworkers soon heard how they'd been fooled and back they charged. Snooty and his pals stood with their backs to the wall, grinning like Cheshire cats. The Gasworkers were big and tough, but Snooty's Gang didn't give that a thought. "Right!" shouted Snooty and his chums dodged cleverly out of the way as the ugly bullies charged.

Have you ever hit a rubber wall at full speed? This one gave the Gasworkers a fright. The wall bent back and back — under the weight of the bullies. Then — PYONNG! — it sprang upright like a ruler firing a pellet and fired the Gasworkers back the way they had come. That shook them! "Ow! That hurts!" The bullies howled.

They'd landed in a thorn bush, that's why! But Snooty and his chums were very kind to the bullies. They removed the thorns from them at a penny a time! "We'll have no more trouble with them today," said Snooty. He was right!

48

the gang get up to lots of tricks!

But having had some fun with the bricks, Snooty and his pals began to think of making something useful with them. "What about building rubber furniture?" said Snooty. "A good idea!" agreed the gang. So they all went to work with glue and hand trowels. It was great fun while it lasted.

Swanky and Thomas made a bed of bricks and a brick pillow and blanket to match. Snatchy made an easy chair — it was easy to make, too! He slapped the rubber bricks together in no time while Snitchy made a rubber foot-rest — for tired feet! Snooty acted as foreman to see there were no slackers.

Then, of course, the gang had to try the furniture out. That was a bit of a snag! For once they tried out the comfy furniture, they didn't want to get up. It was too much like work! But when Snooty hit on the idea of selling their comfy furniture — the gang were on their feet in a flash!

When all the furniture had been tested, Snooty put up notices on the castle wall to attract buyers. "This ought to bring the tired folk along," he said. It wasn't long before some interested customers flocked into the castle to see the amazing furniture. Big folk, thin folk, short and tall!

"All our own work," said Snooty. "Beds, sofas, easy chairs — everything you need in the way of comfy furniture. But don't just take my word for it, try it. Then you'll want to buy it."

Snooty was beaming with pride as he led the way — but you know what comes after pride! A fall! Sure enough, the fun began. Well, it wasn't exactly fun for Snooty and his pals. The customers didn't sit down gently on the furniture. They jumped up and down on it. In half a tick they were being fired round the room like human cannon-balls. Crack! One of them went through the ceiling.

Crunch! Bump! That was another one raising a lump! Whang! Whoof! Another went soaring to the roof. "Ooh!" gulped Snooty.

"We'd have been safer making ordinary furniture like sensible people!" Even Aunt Mat got the fright of her life!

But there wasn't any time to cry over spilt milk! The gang had to get busy giving the customers first-aid for their bruises. And the customers didn't even offer to pay for the sticking plaster and bandages. Aunt Mat had to pay — and she told the gang what she thought of them.

When the customers had gone, Aunt Mat started making out the bill. What with holes in the roof, broken vases — not forgetting the bandages — the total was £20. And Aunt Mat decided to take it off the gang's pocket money. That meant no pocket money till next Christmas! What a thought!

That was a black look-out for the gang. "Rubber bricks!" moaned Snooty. "RUBBER BRICKS! I hate 'em!" So the pals fetched some scissors and began to cut the bricks up into pieces. They enjoyed that. They sliced them, chopped them and cut chunks off them.

Snooty had another plan. They weren't just cutting the bricks up in a temper. Oh, no! They were making them into rubbers to sell. And they sold like hot cakes! Very soon they had enough money to pay Aunt Mat and to buy double helpings of ice cream, too!

Adapted from the original which appeared in 'The Beano Book 1956'.

49

Here's a most unusual thing— a stinging wasp without a sting!

Snooty wants to be the Mayor—
but his opponent won't play fair!

The Beano January 30th, 1943.

Alternative modes of transportation—
cause the old folks great consternation.

The Beano March 27th, 1943.

The Prof's latest smart invention—
leads to trouble, strife and tension!

The Beano April 10th, 1943.

A canteen in the castle's hall—
to feed the troops, our heroes all!

The Beano July 17th, 1943.

Snooty is placed in a tricky situation— thanks to some shady opposition.

The Beano July 31st, 1943.

The townsfolk all run helter-skelter—
straight into the air-raid shelter.

The Beano November 6th, 1943.

The Bunkerton gang produce the goods—
and turn over a pair of hoods.

continued from page 39

7. Snooty was full of bright ideas, but only one in a hundred worked once in a while. So the Gang weren't too enthusiastic as they followed him into town. "At least it gets us away from the hippos for a while!" Scrapper muttered to Joe. "But if I know Snooty he'll get us into worse trouble." Soon Snooty stopped before a shop that made fancy dress and animal costumes. "Here we are," he said. "We're going in."

8. Luckily, Aunt Mat had an account at the shop and Snooty was able to get what he wanted. It was a big order — a full-size hippo costume! Snooty and the girls watched while the others climbed into the costume and headed off toward the Zóo. People looked on pop-eyed when they saw the false hippo coming, then they scattered. They thought it was real!

9. Back at the Zoo, poor Snitchy and Snatchy had been having a terrible time. They had tried to play with the hippos, but the hippos played with them instead, and it was a rough game, too. Snooty and Swanky stood well out of reach while the fake hippo charged towards them. Then Snooty introduced it to the babies as their Ma! Too bad! The hippos weren't fooled one bit. They knew it was a fake!

continued on page 67

Snooty's distinguished family tree—
reveals some Scottish 'ances-tree'.

The Beano February 26th, 1944.

The competition becomes so thrilling—
with a most peculiar sausage filling.

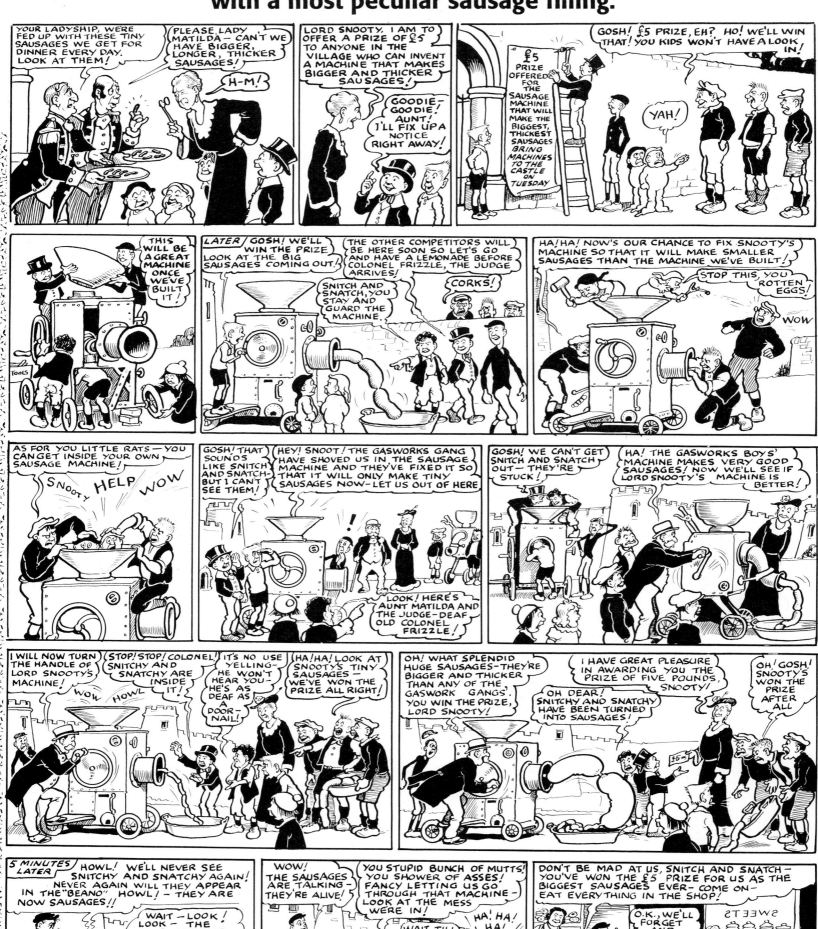

The Beano June 3rd, 1944.

His Lordship's filled with raging ire—
the coupons are upon the fire.

All the apples they can eat—
but who's this new girl on the beat?

The Beano August 12th, 1944.

Young Snooty and the gang's a quiver— they want the boat out on the river.

Hidden treasure is Snooty's inspiration—
but surely there's a more 'soot'-able occupation.

The Beano October 7th, 1944.

Snitchy and Snatchy grab their chance—
to lead the pals a merry dance.

With Gertie gone, his Lordship regrets— his choice of less troublesome pets.

The Beano December 2nd, 1944.

continued from page 58

10. The hippos howled in earnest this time. They thought this was a silly trick. Then, all at once, their tears stopped. The keeper was approaching with their real Ma on a lead. Snooty saw Ma Hippo, too — and he saw the jealous look on her face. "Look out, Gang!" he cried. "Ma Hippo thinks you've been trying to steal her job. She's not pleased at all!" But it was too late. Mother Hippo snorted and charged forward like an army tank.

11. Wham! The real hippo hit the fake hippo. Rrrip! The fake hippo costume split in two, and the Gang tumbled out on the ground. Snooty was knocked over in the commotion. But the Gang had succeeded in making the baby hippos laugh at last. "Isn't our Ma clever?" they were thinking. "She's shown these boys a thing or two." But Snooty and his pals were out for the count.

12. Luckily, the keeper was a good sort. He knew that the boys had only been trying to help, so he fixed them up with a bed in the Zoo hospital. So Snooty, Scrapper, Thomas and Big Fat Joe spent a week in a ward with sick tigers, elephants, snakes and ostriches. And they had to eat the same food as the animals, too. Still, it wouldn't have been so bad if Snitch and Snatch hadn't come every visiting hour to laugh!

Adapted from the original which appeared in 'The Beano Book 1954.'

When Aunt Mat mislays her money—
the way it's found is rather funny!

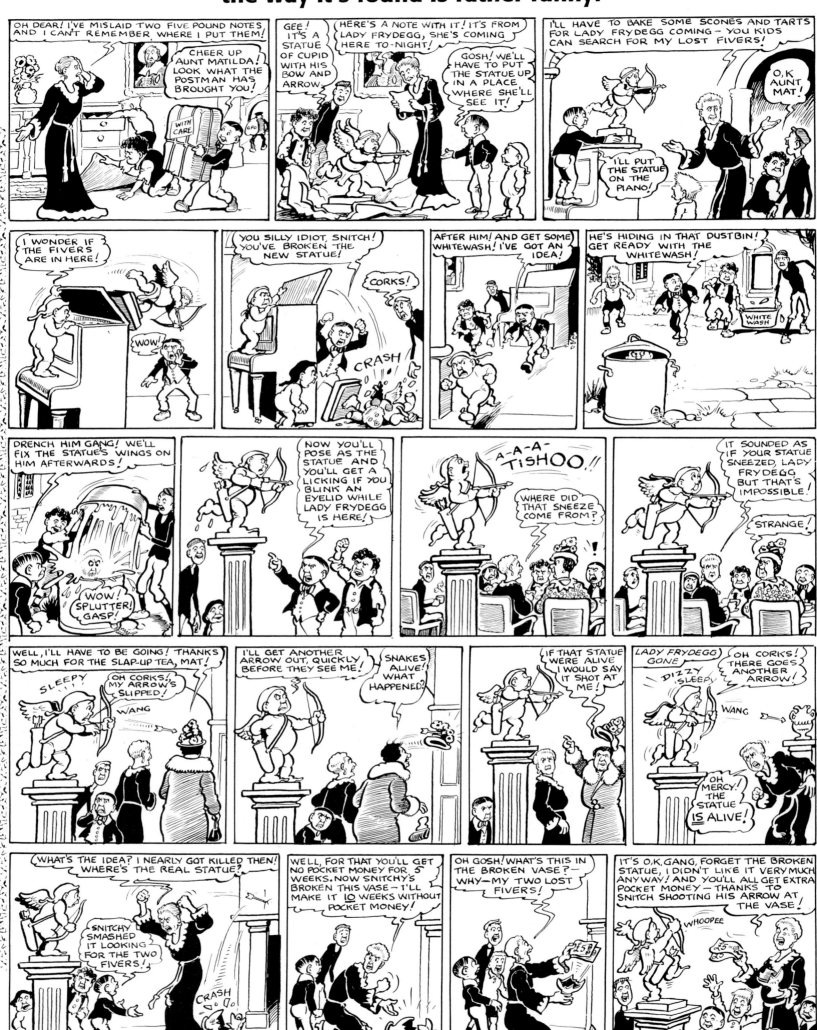

Snitch and Snatch, those little weasels— now pretend they've got the measles!

The Beano March 10th, 1945.

The Gasworks Gang and their misdemeanours—
end up taken to the cleaners.

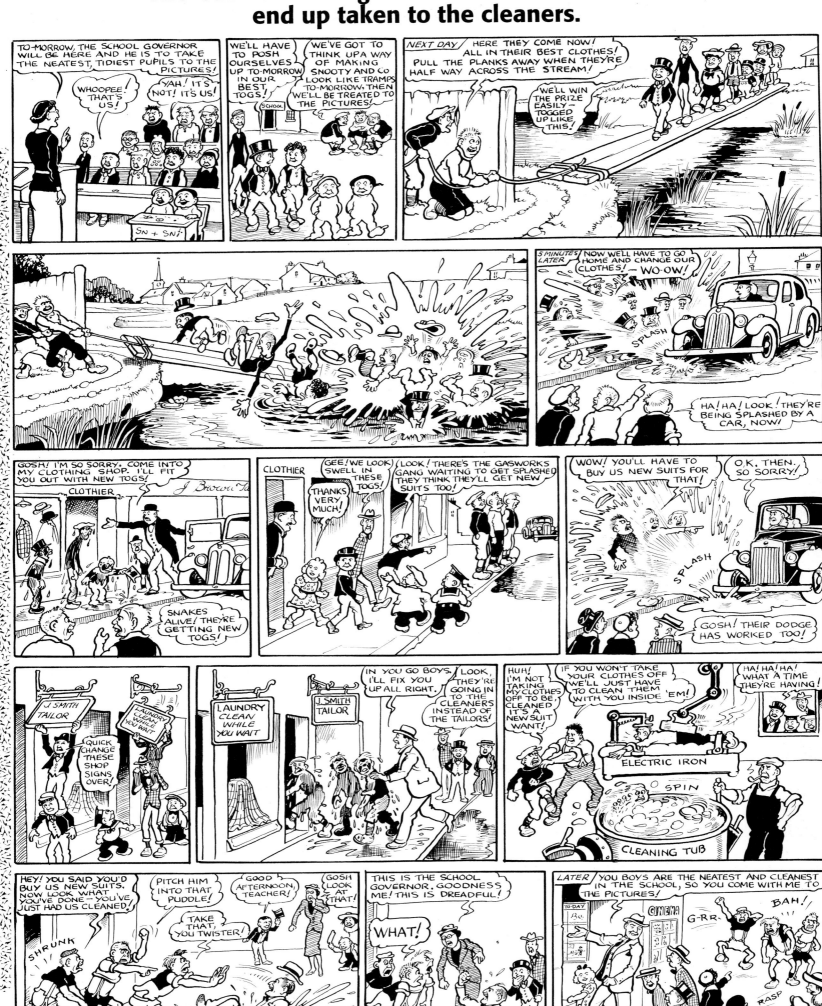

The Beano July 14th, 1945.

A brand new filmshow's on in town— though who can watch it upside down?

The Beano October 6th, 1945.

A Christmas prank is lots of fun—
but it's not merry for *everyone*!

The Beano December 15th, 1945.

A picnic lunch down at the beach—
for Snooty, is just out of reach.

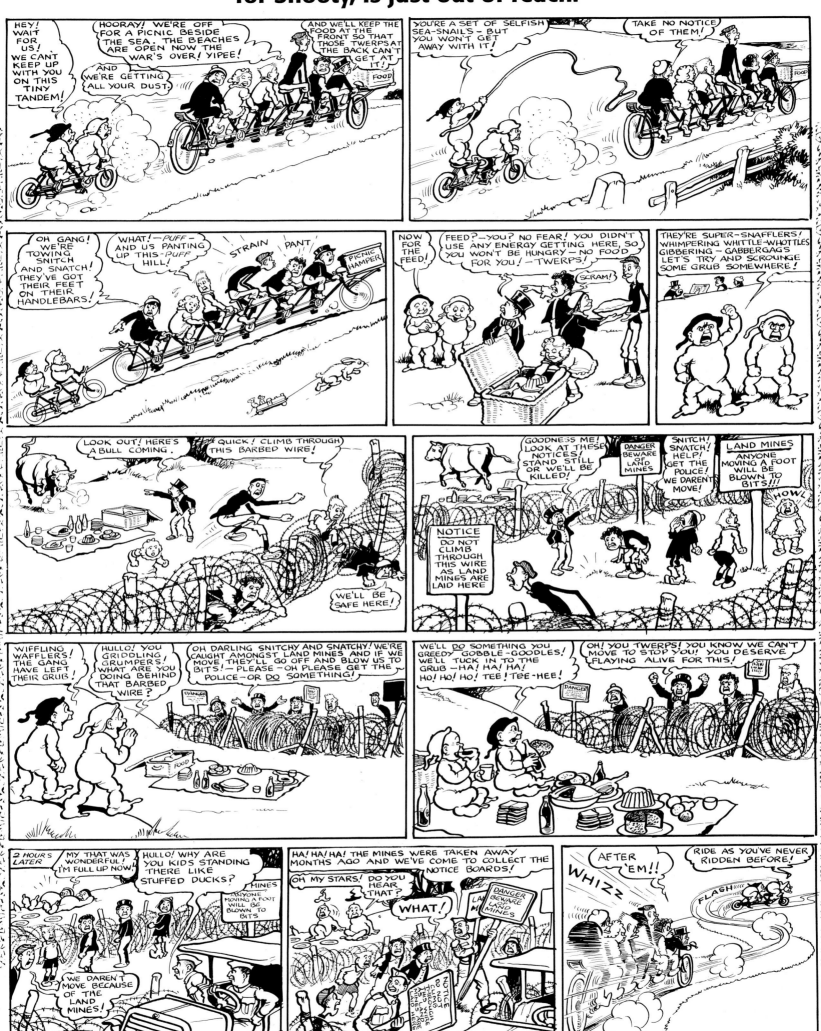

The Beano March 9th, 1946.

When some policemen come to stay—
dirty tricks the boys can't play.

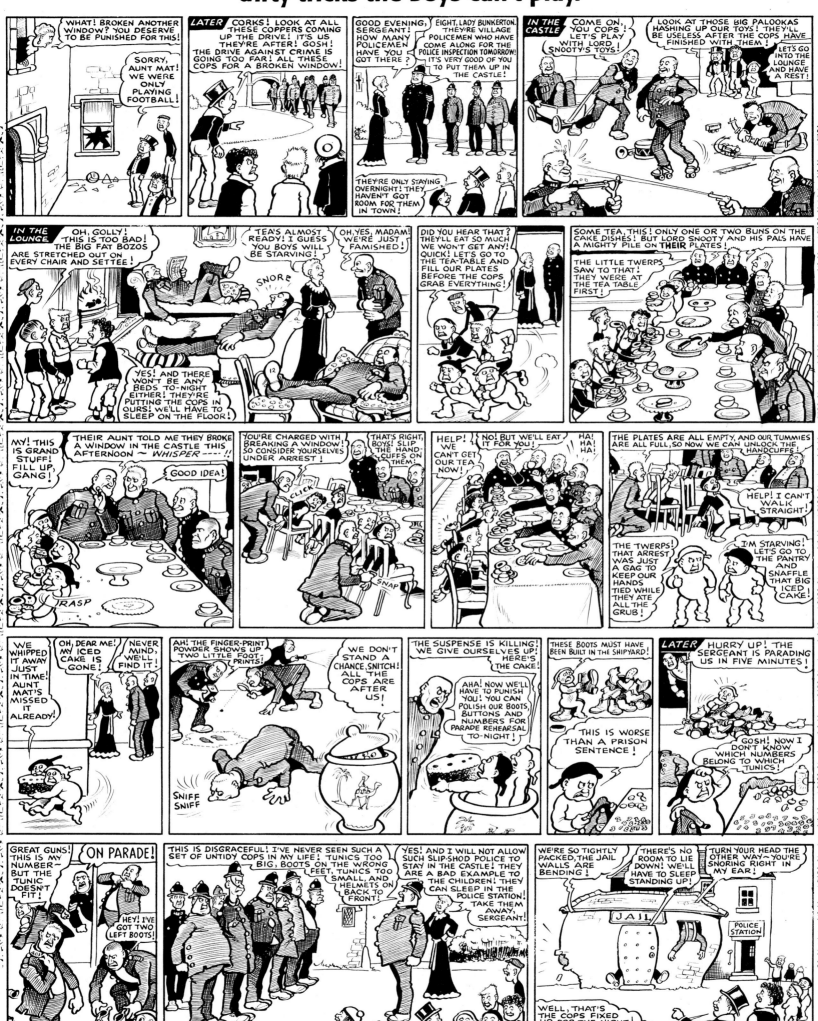

The Beano June 14th, 1947.

Oh, woe! Oh, gosh! Oh, deary me—
Snooty's lost an important key.

The Beano March 5th, 1949.

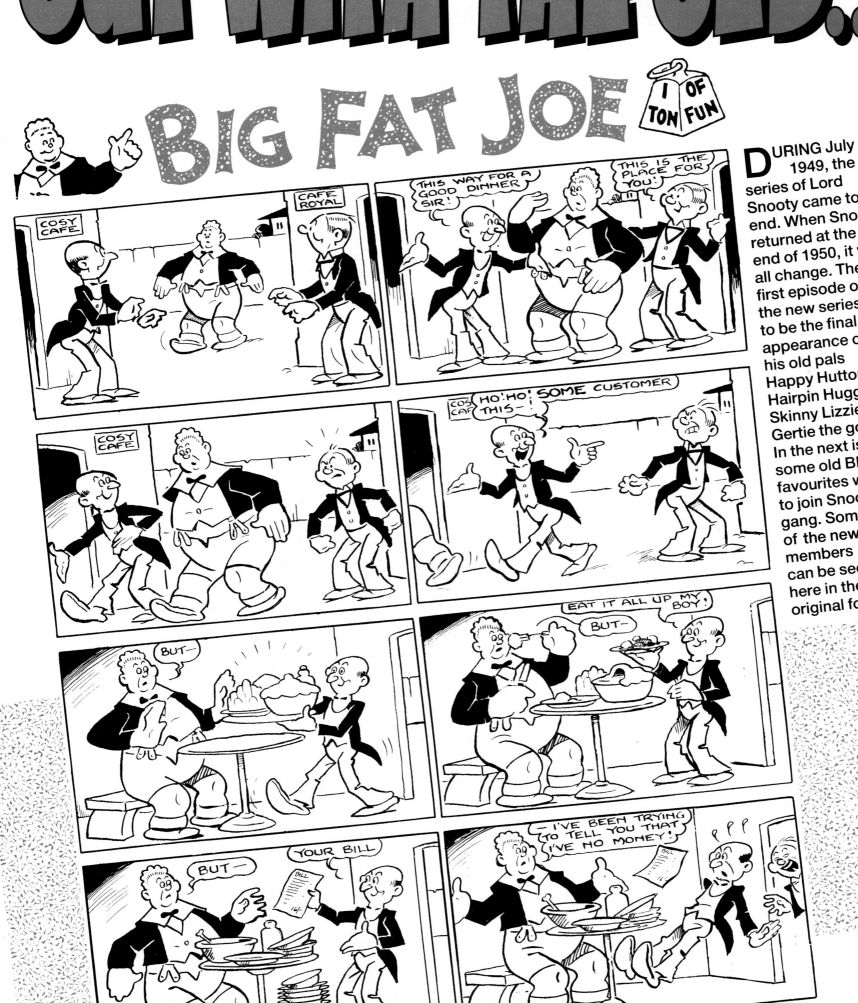

BIG FAT JOE

1 OF TON FUN

DURING July 1949, the first series of Lord Snooty came to an end. When Snooty returned at the end of 1950, it was all change. The first episode of the new series was to be the final appearance of his old pals Happy Hutton, Hairpin Huggins, Skinny Lizzie and Gertie the goat. In the next issue some old BEANO favourites were to join Snooty's gang. Some of the new members can be seen here in their original form.

DOUBTING THOMAS

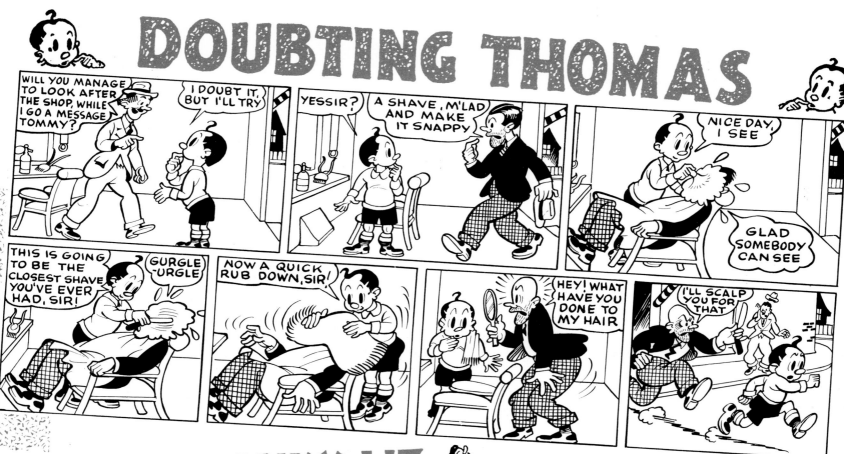

SWANKY LANKY LIZ

Things were to change with the artists, too.

This second series would run till 1958, but not all of the strips were drawn by Dudley Watkins. Albert Holroyd, Robert Nixon and Ken Harrison are amongst the other artists who have illustrated Snooty stories.

However, these were carefully done so that none of the charm and style Watkins had given Lord Snooty was lost.

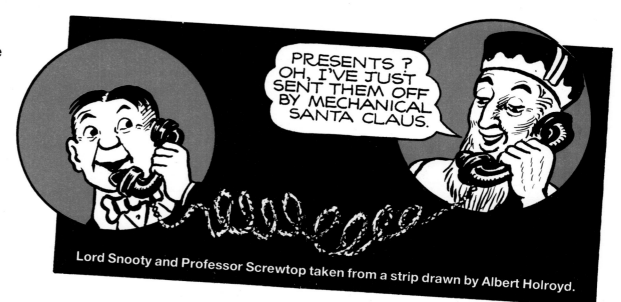

PRESENTS? OH, I'VE JUST SENT THEM OFF BY MECHANICAL SANTA CLAUS.

Lord Snooty and Professor Screwtop taken from a strip drawn by Albert Holroyd.

When Snitch and Snatch each get a double—
it can only mean one thing, that's trouble!

A brand new house is nice and light— but then it vanishes in the night!

The Beano April 26th, 1952.

Snooty's off to fetch some holly— but what a pest he is, by golly.

The Beano December 19th, 1953.

When the gang end up an April fool—
it means a holiday from school.

Snooty helps a penniless friend—
by encouraging the Yanks to spend, spend, spend!

The Beano May 25th, 1957.

The gang pick out a brand new pet—
but they're not too happy with what they get.

The Beano June 1st, 1957.

Aunt Mat gives the gang advice—
don't be fooled and caught out twice.

The Beano May 19th, 1962.

When Thomas thinks it's going to rain—
the clothes he wears are far from plain.

Watch the blades turn round and round—
they're helping Snooty earn a pound.

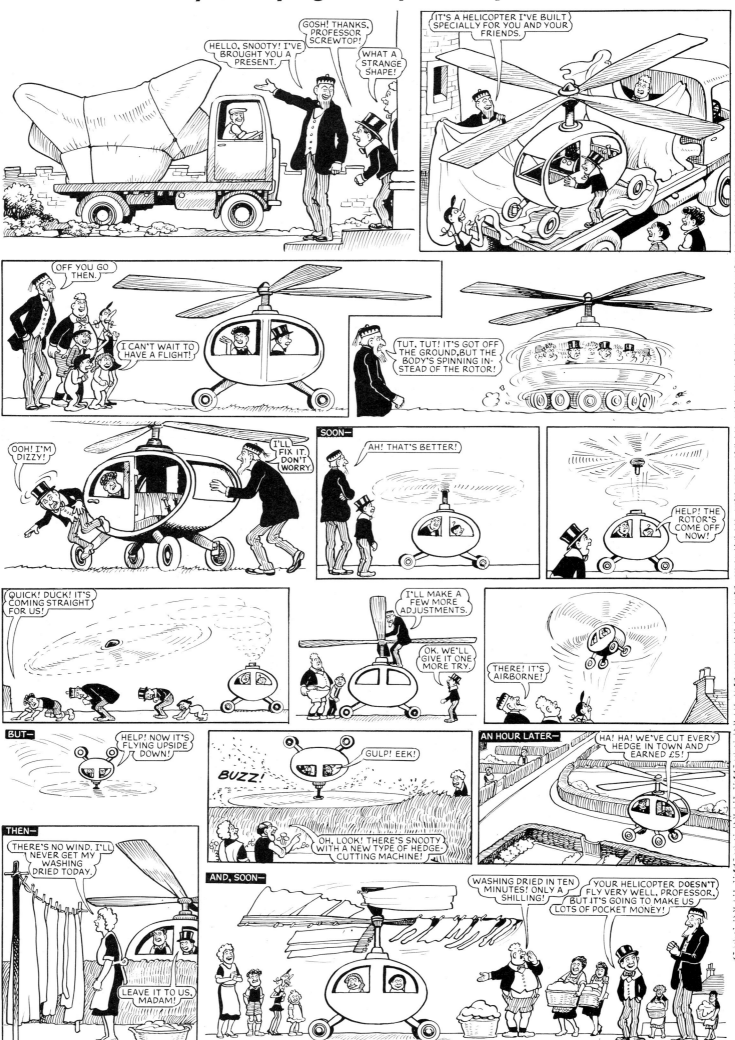

Lots of tricks come into play— when it comes to 'Beano' day.

The Beano March 20th, 1965.

The race is on to see who's best—
in the jam tart eating contest.

The Beano March 19th, 1966.

**The gang are stuck deep in the jungle—
but it seems to be a gardening bungle.**

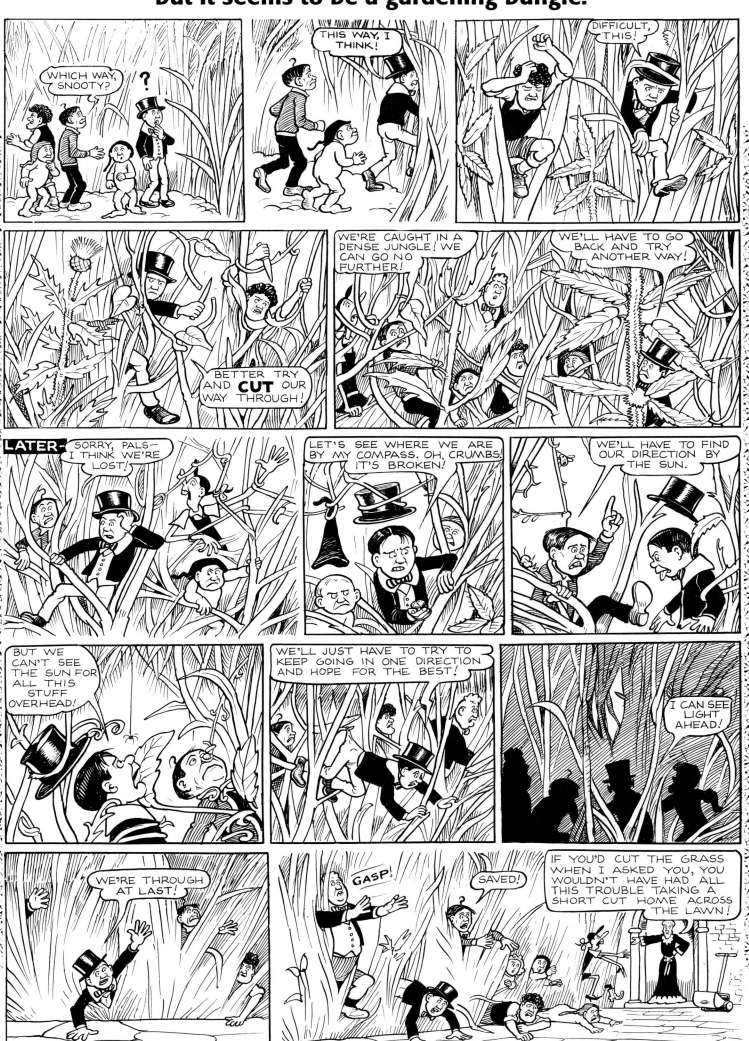

Swanky Liz thinks she's a toff— but soon regrets her showing off!

Snooty sets an alarm clock—
but it's not one that goes tick-tock!

LORD SNOOTY

THIS double page strip is a good example of how Watkins' artwork had changed during the sixties. Although the characters remained the same, the overall look had become more open and modern.

ME TOO! LORD DENNIS

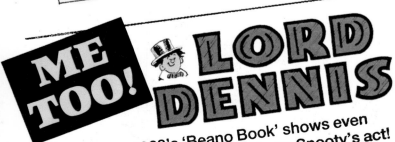

This strip from 1968's 'Beano Book' shows even Dennis the Menace trying to get in on Snooty's act!

Adapted from the original.

Printed and Published in Great Britain by D. C. Thomson & Co., Ltd., 185 Fleet Street, London EC4A 2HS.

 ISBN 0-85116-691-1

Adapted from the original which appeared in 'The Beano Book 1969'.